To:

From:

Dedication:

FOUR SEASONS OF DREAMS

Elisa-Nefeli

AN ALBEDO PROJECT SOCIETY PUBLICATION ©
© 2022 ELISA- NEFELI

All Rights Reserved

Unauthorized translation, duplication , photocopying, introduction or distribution partially or fully, under any means, including electronic copying, storage or distribution is a violation of applicable laws. Albedo Project Association is a logo owned by Albedo Project Library all rights reserved.The moral right of Elisa-Nefeli, to be identified as the Author, this work has been asserted in the accordance With the Copyright Designs and Patents Act of 1998All rights reserved. No part of this publication my be reproduced,
Stored in a retrieval system, or transmitted in any form or by any means, electronic, mechanical, photocopying, recording, or otherwise, without the prior permission of both the copyright owner and the above publisher of this work.All the characters in this composition are fictitious, and any resemblance to actual persons, living or dead, is purely coincidental.

Table of Contents

Acknowledgment i
About the Author ii
Important Note iv
Introduction 1
Morning at the Island 6
Voyage 8
Pilgrimage 11
Notes 13
Awakening 16
Happiness 19
A Surrealist Summer Dream 20
How Many Stars Do You Hold? 24
Magus 32
Impressions 38
Fearless 41
The Origami Of My Dream 44
Glossary 50

Acknowledgment

A special acknowledgment to the Amazon Pros team for their help in making this book a reality.

About the Author

Having experienced the hardship of a dictatorship at an early age Elisa-Nefeli decided for a life of action. She advanced in medical studies and the humanities, excelled in different sports and worked in projects relating to arts education self betterment. She lived across four continents between the West the Far East and Asia. She started writing from an early age. She sees Poetry as painting through words and sharing new vistas.

FOUR SEASONS OF DREAMS

Important Note

In a literary work, to have the full grasp of its message, it has been observed, that it is important to understand the meaning of the words as used in it especially in poetry. For that there is a simple Glossary at the end of the book which defines the words used by the author in a simple way to assist you get a better understanding of the content of the poems. This does not replace the utilization of a proper dictionary when available to help you grasp fully the concepts being communicated.

Introduction

"Four Seasons of Dreams" was written as a simple expression of an inner world. It was created, to assert a freedom of formulation against material vectors and sometimes oppressive limitations.

Having survived a dictatorship, having seen a lot of viciousness, and having first hand reality of what true hardship is, it has been my way to wish for a new, better future.

That creation, kept me connected to what I am, away from any invitations of hate and away from any temptation of wanting to "get even" with suppression and injustice. I do consider that the moment you agree with such attitudes and such desire, you end up in the "same pot" with ways and attitudes you protest against.

That viewpoint has been my compass to a way out. A way that gives fodder to courage, affinity, imagination, entertain-ment and power.

I created these poems as a reminder of what we truly are, an insistence to keep the elation of creating, unscathed, from any low and dark aspects that an existence in the material may bring.

It is overall, a declaration that there is a sunny side and nurturing nature in people, in life, without having to close one's eyes to how things are realistically speaking.

It is above all, inspired and dedicated to those people, who are great enough to not give in, to any force of oppression but keep up to their greatness and determination to help the living.

This work takes in account all opposite and complementary situations that human nature entails including those vital factors that act as an antidote to the crude force of the physical universe – imagination and joy of creation.

You can find this work as a collection, but it the near future you some single poems will be made available. At the end of this book you will find my "Concise Manual On Poetry". It some experiences and some tips which I wanted to share with you from my journey into the creation of "Four Seasons of Dreams". The "Concise Manual" is made as well available for you as a separate publication. The concept, in creating those shorter editions, was, that you could offer them to someone you think may benefit from them.

At the end of this book you will find a space where you can express your own "Four Seasons of Dreams" and then simple Glossary where some words are defined as intended in the composition.

With all that said, I want to thank you for being you, as each person in its own way contributes to further cultural exchange, as a reader and as a creator.

I kindly ask you to keep your dreams and creations going, keep your thirst for betterment and keep adding aesthetics to life.

I wish you enjoy these "paintings" of living moments and ideas created through words. After all poetry originally means simply - a creation.

Elisa- Nefeli

"Dedicated to those, who work hard,

to cast their dreams in real life.

DREAMS
AT SPRING

Morning at the Island

By the balustrade
I see the morning
approaching slowly
carried by a clear
blue sky

I see her coming
up the stone made
stairs

On her shoulder
she carries
a wicker basket
full of fruits
full of colours
full of songs
canary and nightingales
all around her
naughty sparrows
and light

She sees me
she hugs and kisses
full of joy
to what is real
she pulls a curtain
She sits herself
carefully upon a chair
asks for butter and honey
on handmade bread
and a cold brew
medium with milk

As I serve her
I meet her eyes
I become one with
that perception
one with that essence

One with the colours
and rhythm
that feels island
full of life
full of giving
and morning adventure

Voyage

The hour when the shadows grow,
a voyage,
the evening lowers
its eyelashes to the light

Zephyr breaths,
his caress
a dance to the roses,
a rustling
on their petals.

The trifling walk
on the dusty road
till the thin line
of the horizon

A Voyage

A crimson whisper
my thoughts
that follow the sunset

Nothing approaching
nothing distancing
and all that was summoned
by forms
a delicate ripple
upon serenity
Sounds of faces,
Sounds of memories

With all what we experienced
as our luggage
our essence blossoms
and opens
to the dawning glare
inciting our shadows
to mature

A voyage

A delicate dance
our life
in a sun tanned dream
reveals itself
while the sunset
casts its eyes
to the light

Upon its body
the waves
reach and withdraw
like the rhythm
of life

Listen

Upon the
blue and white water
of moments that rise
and shift

Upon the tumbling
waves of time

Upon matter that
converts through
spirit and creation

Through winds
that change a fate
with every tack
of an existence

Life
is a voyage

Pilgrimage

In the passage of the day
needless the thoughts
and if you play with words
as well needless

The day is brought forth
by the silence of a night
and the sun expands
and follows

The most beautiful poem
a child
a kite
and their diversion

A pilgrimage that runs
after dreams with laughter

Tend your hand
cast the dance
the most beautiful colour
will initiate it
step by step
one step forward
one backward
and then a round and about

The time has come
to end
that nothing but
the loving of dreams

The time has come
to paint
till it springs
what you want
to be real

The most beautiful poem
a child
an apple
that turquoise of the sky
that promises their voyage

Tend your hand
cast the dance
the most beautiful colour
will initiate it

Notes

With youthful notes
I painted a unique world

A brand-new original world

With an ivory piano
I founded
an untouched furtive
music

That flutters in the
light blue azure of my mind
and reaches even wider

And it is golden
like the gold
of a spring day

And it is blue
like the breath
of a sea
in a turquoise moment

With novel words
I leisured
there
away from cacophony
and spite

So transparent and small

Adjoined to a world
that poises crystalline
and placid

And it is golden
like a sun
of a spring day

And is gentle
like the inspiration
of a sea
at a blue day

With untouched colours
I bargained
a blue understanding

By paying for ransom
these words

And so I prevailed
in a new young world

DREAMS IN SUMMER

Awakening

Upon the lips of a dream
stood the eminent kiss
the flicker of a star
became a wish

Golden the smile
that awoke slowly
like the gentle scent
that sleeps besides me

Awakening

Outside the window
the breathing of the wind
touched me
serene
summer like
to then move on
to broaden
on a frame of the day

Gentle the breeze
that warmly reaches within
and caresses my essence
the Being I am
in a golden dance

Gentle

The hay at the field
stretched
and looked at me
once from here
and once from there

That placid motion
follows the mind
at peace as far as the horizon
that dressed itself
with morning

Awakening

Nature
became now
an oriental
dancer

Dressed in vivid
colours
readied to dance
the belly dance
of a sunrise

She moves her hips
puts life on fire

Resembles a promise
full of passion
full of expectancy

She looks around
with an alluring gaze
resolute
fearless
she kindles the rhythm
she incites the motion
she sweats a blossoming scent
as she ripples out life
she silently calls out
that urge for living

And nature
Like a dervish
Turns ecstatic
and follows

Happiness

Upon your shoulder lightly
Rests, and refreshes the summer
And you have the power
to look at the crimson
straight in the eye
and flutter its draft

Like the dance of the sun ray
upon summer leafs
like the rhythm of the dream
at the concert of the night

Even when the shadows of some fun
cease to be those of a child
upon the grey looks of this road

You have the power
The flicker of the hour
to yet mold
And to sail away and laugh

You have the power

And when you set your sails
You do not forget

To keep by the power
a freshness
an afternoon freshness
and its impression

A Surrealist Summer Dream

From upon the shoulders
of a night
the sun
shook and tended
his hair golden

He stared at me
he gazed fire
he gently touched me
like a victory of life
that awakes
and takes form

From his hair
an infinity of sun rays
travelled hundreds of miles
to reach space

As soon as they
land
they dress vividly
and spread around the old house
like rule-less children

They dash into the kitchen
giggling
cupboards they open
cupboards they close
to find butter cookies
and coffee

And I follow
barely awake
for that golden treat

The small burner
they lighten
with an ancient golden match
they count in gold some sugar
they measure cup and water

They launch the "dance"
in a copper coffee pot

This is their way
they say
this is my way

"Come, come"
come with us to sip perception
Come
to be filled with our sunny side
One sip
one taste
one day
A Fragrance
a Sea
a Sun
a Sky
those sun rays all about
and my white bed sheets

A painting of Life
A vision ahead
a breathing sea
expands in blue
full of freshness
full of life

Far and away
the waves raise their height
and chant in holy crests
what is to come

I blow the hour
dash and smile
I dress of no worry
as I look at a freshly painted
morning

DREAMS IN AUTUMN

How Many Stars Do You Hold?

How many stars do you hold?

You, that hold in your eyes
the night's velvet vision?

How many stars do you hold?

How many stars approached
for you to listen?

How many stood by you
close enough to perceive them?

And if the night was needless
of your dream
she came by you
unexpected
upon a dark line of the horizon
stunning
to experience you
without any display

It was then that you
perceived her
the way she perceived you
throughout
and you became one

And if through stars
her depth you discovered
like a moonlight
pulsing
like moonlight
she mirrored
your gentle light within

Then you could savour her
and emerged as one
with her satin like texture

You became
one with the sunrise

You matured
and permeated all

Through the door
of my mind's
most secret door
from end to end
you discerned me
in a light and tender
moment

How many stars do you hold?

And while the silence
poems whispered
could you catch them?

How many stars do you hold?

You that know
how to sail and expand life
how to kiss the Zephyr
upon the rustling of leaves
how to make him
draft a sigh
to remind you

How many stars do you hold?
You painted beauty
on my dreams
casting them
from the intangible
in truth

In that groove
our summers grew
like a deep breath
afore the tide

Like footprints on sand
that were swept away
and remained therefore
upon it forever

How many stars do you hold?

How many paces, upon sand
life became?

Her fever brought
vim upon our body

And we exchanged our being
and moved on to our tomorrow
with a new perception
which is a bit of you
and a bit of me

How many stars do you hold?

You that hold
within your sight
that nightly velvet?
How many stars
you bent to a kiss

I am here to remind you
close to a sound of African Bongos
resembling the sound of a sea

Near a crimson sunset
that gently awakes the night

How many stars do you hold?

Like a Pirate
upon the body of
my mind you sail

Laden with ancient
treasures
hidden
in legendary dreams

Riches that resemble
innocent castles
cast on a sandy beach

Castles made out
the sands of time
that sparkle like glass
under the sun

That emerge solid
even if they are
an ephemeral
children's dream
Castles
that on the forever
you assembled
to then sweep them away
in a silent hour

You turned them into
a far and away past
that rides
a deep blue sea

Warped them
into games
transformed them
into passion
emerged them as waves
that reach
and withdraw
alike meanders
awaiting
my existence

Waves
which are blue
and are white
which are yesterday
and today
which are also
a tomorrow

How many stars do you hold?

How many footsteps, upon sand
you did not want
to repeal
to the swell of life

How many dreams
upon the shoulders of my sun
that expanded and shone
resembling sun rays
gold
unruly

How many stars do you hold?

Echo of the horizon
painter of the hour

How many stars do you hold?
How many?

And if you disguised them
to expose them
you do not ow
in the now
or in any evermore

Just close your eyes
and I will follow

DREAMS
IN WINTER

Magus

You are the Magus of devotion
fold your eyes
clear your dream

You are the creator
of a moment
that touches my being
and starts the world

You are
a classic image
of fascination
upon your hand
a magic wand
upon your lips
a diverse spell
that signals power
that quiets the night

I came to grasp you
through life
to bring you upon wind
upon sensation
to have you here
with me
for ever

I came
to lead you
to a moment
of fairy tales
from the once upon a time
to the tick of this instant

There
where you can rise
far and away
forget yourself
deliver yourself
right here right now
into the don't
and the forever

You are the dimension
of the dream
in whose scent
I wanted to dress on
to learn with
to define from

You are a desire
that pulses within
and I came
to spend you
from end to end
with a caress

You will then discern me
from that high up window
your magic castle holds
how I flutter and rise
laughing like a child
gliding
pursuing
forests and dusty roads
that lead and end
in your enchanted world

As a Magus
you will peruse
every secret
like a Magus
you will perceive
you will experience
the way I am
bereft of social masquerades
the way I am
beyond the shadows
of make believe

You will perceive me
you will know me
throughout
in the upside
and the downside
in light
and in darkness

In the earthly
in the magic
you will know
how to treasure me

You will know

How to undress
from the ordinary
my mind
how to suit her
in dreams
in magic

You are the Magus of devotion
fold your eyes clear your dream

Spell the fancy
to appear
and so find me
know me
live me

And all which
afore the know
remained secret
will now be spelled
fair and shiny
through the crystalline
to the transparent
of my ways

And so be it
that I will bare
your magic dimension
I will bare all colours
even the deepest
for you to see
for you to experience

And know me
throughout
in the upside
and the downside
in the humdrum
or the light
in the illusion
or the forthwith
all the way
unto another dimension
of the essence within

You are the Magus of devotion
fold your eyes clear your dream

You are the Magus
the Magus...
the Magus...

THE OTHER SEASONS OF DREAM

Impressions

Life
That blossoms
the hour of the sun

Zest that broadens
Colour and motion
ambition

Vigour
that thereafter
shrinks
turns into sand and dust

I reach to hold it
yet it slides
amid my mortal fingers
it dissolves
it expires
into some yesterday

And if for a moment
the meaning escaped me
I found it again
right here
at this lonely seashore

I created her newly
besides a calm sea
white and blue
to sail me gently
toward my fantasy

I let thought to dress
in wind and surf
the white mane
of their crest

Idea to carry me
from the unknown
to this margin
of space

A space
that embraces
that tinkles
from narrow borders
till an immense look
of the horizon

Impressions
moments

You feel them permeate
every inch of this texture
you feel them reach within
and as you perceive them
your wealth grows in spirit
and you wake up
from an eternal sleep
of material
into the essence
of who you are
of what you are

And you chant
the now and forever
as you resurrect

The wind advances
does not wait
his presence drafts
through scattering moments
like specks of sand
like mists of time
No
it does not hurt

Not any more
as nothing comes
and nothing goes

when you are wind
when you know
when you are you
aware of your every moment
Yes you say what for?
It does not last
The moment maybe not
but the know of it
will be with you forever

Fearless

Under a crescent moon
fearless I could sleep
The sun crackled
while burning the wood besides me
sparkling at dusk
a fire within

The waters in the river
full of vision
they flowed
their gurgling waters
cleaned in passing
the wounds of times past

The winds from the forest
were the trees speak the runes
filled me with life
and life flowed
till the edge of my fingers
through a pen that leads to the sea
made of paper
and colourful ink
that unite and sing the hymn of concepts

Through the ashes
of my imagination
I grew again
like the legend of the Phoenix
where an end is a beginning

By dawn as fearless wings
upon my thoughts grew
the conformist control forces
appeared
with an arrest warrant
to take away my dreams

But could they actually see them?

My life they wanted to place
in a cage
to exhibit it
at a zoo of arts
for their young to look at
and learn not to dare this tune

But when they opened their hands
they found them empty
my song I sang
a song that sat me free

I offered them the fruit of knowledge
the essence of life
but they said they could not stand
its peels and its nuts
they were conformists

I offered them some understandings
but they thought it worthless
as it had no price tag

I offered them peace and redemption
but they said there was nothing to redeem from
the bullets and bombs
and all human suffering
they are a boys game
like a monopoly

I filled my backpack then
full of words
I filled my bottle
with creation
to end my thirst

I rode the clouds
to arrive by a forest
full of butterflies
and kids
to nurture the living
to help the blind see
to climb in action
stairs that lead
to where your life
truly lives

The Origami Of My Dream

Upon the lips
of a dream
red lipstick
the sunset spread

It revolved
and stared at me
in gold

With its orange colour
the hour ticked

A fluff I collected
of white cloud
and a fountain pen
filled with water falls
to mark my being
within this moment

In a timeless bit
I cast
fold by fold
a structure
an Origami ship
made of east
made of colour

A tiny paper boat
small and vivid
to sail me
peacefully
on those
smiley lips
of fancy

Upon the blue
of a sea
I carefully deliver it
to drift on it gently

On its bridge
I wrote
"Have a good trip"
and "May God provide"

Upon its stern
I painted
a little mermaid

As the ship
distances
with a delicate bob
I saw her
looking ahead
proud and strong

Her tail curled
her chest straight
her hair a crest
of salt and satin

As she sailed
I saw her
calling for laud
at the seagulls

They rose white
as they flew past
they chanted her
sealing her beauty
in a seagull psalm

I let it go
free
upon a picture
of an immense
turquoise

I let it sail
with direction
my unknowns
with compass
my tomorrows
Small fragile
but also great
like a future

I grow through it
perceiving

I feel it
as it sails
how it bobs lightly
toward deep waters
toward
that profound and scary indigo
small but dauntless

like my composite
existence

It sails stably
it weaves
slowly
calmly
stern and certain
to the immensity
ahead

But even if small
I saw it standing
knightly
resolute

Great like a virtue
that pulses comfort
Crimson like an intention
Bright and elegant
like a Japanese gift

In its delicate motion
it spells
the "Ds" of dreams
from within me

Light
like a Zephyr
in an afternoon
that caresses
imperceptibly
and salty
as it passes

till triumph
till peace

And it sails on
bobbing
and dashing
here and there
to see it all
to live it all

It's sail
full of wind
climbing or descending
in a straight forward
direction

Pull the sheet
anchors
hang upon the sky
a paper moon
with life for Captain
with compass
intention and mind

With waves for moments

Sail through
discover new lands
in the mundane
or mythical alike
Mark that fantasy
with the tick and tack of
every while
that sails by

And when at sunset
through orange
the hour gazes
through me

Wind
carries me
with it
in crimson
and gold
serene aspirations

Sounds
become whispers
as its tiny deck sways
the rhythm of living
it leaves a pattern
a marked direction
a life
a small
and colourful
Origami ship

Glossary

ADJOINED: Connected or in contact with the word derives from middle French (the language spoke in France between the year 1300 up to the year1500.
Join and ad (together).

AFRICAN BONGOS: One of the pair of small tuned drums played by beating the fingers. The word has its origin in the African Bantu language and it is thought of deriving from their word "mongu" which means and antelope.

AFORE: Before

APPRECIATE: When you consider or give value to something or you are thankful for

ASPIRATIONS: Strong desire, or ambition

AUTHOR: A person who writes a novel, poem or essay

AUBURN: A colour which is between brown and gold or between brown and red.

AZURE: That blue that a clear and unclouded sky has

BALUSTRADE: A railing in a balcony, that barrier in a balcony which has, a horizontal rail, supported by uprights which are widely spaced in between. In that case the upright is what we call a baluster a symmetrical support that widens toward the bottom.

BARGAINED: To make an advantageous purchase after a negotiation or to come to an agreement after negotiation.

BARE: Open to view reveal

BELLY DANCE: A specific solo dance that a woman performs with her middle part of her body exposed that emphasizes movements of the abdominal muscles or pelvis. The dance has its origins to the Middle East.

BENT: directed, inclined or stolen in this context

BEREFT: A simple past tense of bereave which means deprived, without.

BIG CAT: Lions, Tigers, Panthers etc are addressed sometime as Big Cats

BLOSSOMING: A made up word. From Blossom which means the state of flowering and -ing a suffix which shows the action or condition. In the context it means the scent that flowers give out when they blossom open up.

BOB: To move up and down. In the context would indicate the motion of a ship that goes up and down with the motion of the sea.

BUNDLE: Several objects or a quantity of material gathered or bound together.

BRUTALITY: The quality of being cruel or savage being inhuman or acting in a n animal way.

CACOPHONY: Harsh not harmonious. Characterized by a meaningless and dissonant mixture of sounds.

CARRY: To sustain or support something. It includes the concept of transport from one plane to another.

CARRY ON: To continue something like live or work or forwarding an idea despite a setback or tragedy.

CAST: When you form something into a particular shape. When you say "cast its eyes" in that sense it means to direct the eyes or a glance especially in a cursory manner. When you say "cast the dance" you start a dance in turns and twists (like when you dance).

CAST AWAY: To reject to throw away or discard

CASTING: One of the meanings of casting is the act or process of choosing actors to play the various roles in a theatrical production or motion picture. The use of the word in this work indicates that someone chooses something or someone to play a role.

CREATION: The act of producing or causing to exist. The word can be used as in the introduction to mean the original product of the mind, especially an imaginative, artistic work.

CREST: The foamy top of a wave. Or when someone speaks of one's crest on a human being it means long and thick or rough hair. In animals like a horse it means the hair of the horse.

COLLECTION: The gathered or exhibited works of a single painter writer etc.

COMPOSITE: Made up of distinct in kind, essentially different or dissimilar or separate parts or elements compound together.

COMPOSITION: The act of combining parts of elements to form a whole. The resulting product. A literary work.

CONTRIBUTE: Help to cause something. An important factor.

COURAGE: The spiritual or mental quality that backs up a person to face difficulty.

CONTENDING: To compete in opposition, strive in debate

CONVERTS: To modify something so as to serve a different function

CREATIVE: Having the quality or power of creating. Resulting from originality of thought expression, imaginative

CRIMSON: Deep purplish-red color. Sanguinary color

CRYSTALLINE: Clear and transparent like crystal

CULTURE: That which is considered excellent in the arts, manners. A particular form or stage of civilization it can be for a nation in a specific time

DAWNING GLARE: Dawning means the daybreak or start of the day. Glare bright dazzling light. That means that point of the dawn where the sun light becomes bright.

DEBASE: To reduce in value, to lower in dignity

DERVISH: A dervish is a member of various Muslim ascetic order. Some of these orders carry some observances such as dancing energetically and whirling or chanting. In the poem there is an imaginary parallel with the energetic swirling dancing and the energy with which life can begin.

DEVOTION: Profound dedication as well as attachment to a person or cause. The word means as well the assignment of wealth or work to a purpose or cause or a person. Synonyms are affection allegiance dedication adoration.

DISCERNED: To perceive and distinguish mentally or through sight recognize as different.

DISPLAY: Without any show off or exhibiting

DIVERSION: A distraction from care or business a recreation amusement, a pastime

DOWNSIDE: A discouraging or negative aspect

DRAFT: Here it is used to portray a current of air that moves upward or downward

DICTATORSHIP: A government or a form of governement in which absolute power is exercised by a dictator

DISCOVER: To notice or realize. To see to get knowledge of, learn of, about something previously unseen or unknown.

DISCERN: To recognize, distinguish mentally recognize as different. To recognize as distinct.

DIVERSE: Something that is made out of a variety of things, various or manifold.

EARTHLY: Earthly means happening in the material world not in the spiritual realm.

ELATION: is a feeling or emotion of great happiness and excitement about something that has happened or when you do something

EMINENT: something that is above the rest but also that attracts your attention as better

ENHANCE: To enhance something means to improve its value, quality, or attractiveness. Make it better than it was

ECSTATIC: If you are ecstatic, you feel very happy you are full of excitement about something or as an attitude.

ENCHANTED: Means under a spell but also when you are fascinated about something

EPHEMERAL: Something ephemeral is something which is passing which is short lived does not last long

ESSENCE: the characteristic or intrinsic feature of a thing, which determines its identity; fundamental nature the uncheangeable part of something

EXISTENCE The fact or action of being existing

EXPECTANCIES: something which is anticipated the feeling or hope that something exciting, interesting, or good is about to happen

FASCINATION: The quality of creating powerful attraction, charm, magic.

FANCY: Imagination or fantasy that is of deep interest as well as sensual love or deep interest in something as art etc.

FLICKER: Unsteady flame or light like that of a star or of a candle etc

FLUTTERS: That vibrates that moves in that way like the wind when it makes the leafs move with a flapping movement

FLUTTER: To flap the wings rapidly, fly with flapping movements

FLUFF: Light particles as of cotton a soft and light mass

FODDER: coarse food composed of raw material entire material

FORTHWITH: Immediately at once with no delay. In the sense is used is more meaning the "now" the immediate present.

FORMULATION: A method something assembled

FRAGRANCE: A pleasant scent

FRAPPE COFFEE: A cold coffee cold made like a milkshake which has been very popular in Greece it is made with highly soluble grains of coffee especially made for that

FULFILLED: will have carried out or realized a promise or an intention

FORETELLING: To tell before hand predict give a prophesy about something

FUN: enjoyment or a joyous playfulness

FURTIVE: elusive secret

GAZE: to look in a steady and intense manner as if with great interest or wonder

GAZED: It looked in a steady and intense manner with an intent look

GIGGLE: to laugh in a silly juvenile way sometimes when a child has an ill concealed amusement about something

GROOVE: a long and narrow track or channel made to direct the water. It also means in a slang way to appreciate and enjoy immensely. In the text is a mixture of the two indicating a specified direction and enjoyment of one's time

GRASP: to get hold of mentally to comprehend to understand thoroughly or to master

GREEK COFFEE: Is what is also called Arabic Coffee. A specific way to ground and prepare coffee that has its roots in the Middle East where the coffee is cooked and it expands and foams when is ready. There is a thick remain at the bottom. It has become customary in Greece to stir and reverse the remains. In that way at the bottom of the coffee there are some marks that stay from the coffee and "read" some sort of foretelling out of this.

HARDSHIP: The condition of something that is difficult to endure, suffering

HEED: To give careful attention to your careful attention

HOLD: To keep in the hand, to have, support, to own, keep in a specified state or relation, keep in mind. To remain attached or faithful to something. It means as well to have a controlling force or dominate over something

"HOMO SAPIENS": The species to which modern humans belong. The term points out more the species than the spiritual and creative aspect of those who evolved from the species. It is said that this species appeared on planet earth 200,000 years ago

HUMDRUM: Routine, monotony, something dull and boring

IDEA: any concept or conception existing in the mind as the result of mental understanding awareness or activity. A plan of action or intention.

IMAGINE: To create mental images of something not actually present to the senses.

IMPRESSION: A strong effect produced on the intellect, feelings, conscience etc.

INCITING: to urge to prompt into action to encourage

INDIGO: A blue color that can range from deep violet blue to a dark grayish blue

INHERENT: existing in someone or something as a permanent element, or permanent quality or attribute

INHUMAN: Not suitable to human beings, lacking warmth or compassion synonym to cruel or brutal

INITIATE: begin, get going, originate

INNATE: inherent or essential part of the character of something. Something coming from the mind in its natural state rather than learning from educational means or from experience

INSPIRATION: A spiritual quality that animates action or influences action. The result of being filled with an animating and exalting influence. Be filled with a specified feeling or thought.

INTANGIBLE: incapable of being perceived by the sense of touch belonging to something immaterial

INTERACT: to interchange between and act between one and another to communicate with, work with someone or something

INTRIGUE: an attitude or way that brings forth the curiosity or interest on a person by unusual or new or appealing quality to captivate one's curiosity or attention

IVORY: A hard white colour like colour like that of the keys of the piano or similar keyboard instrument.

KINDLES: Kindle means to start something, like a fire. It means also to animate to get going to make bright or illuminate. Kindles is referring to a third person doing that.

LADEN: To be loaded to be filled of

LAUD: To praise a song or hymn that is made to praise someone or something. When you call for is as if you ask you want to cause the praise by someone else

LEGEND: A non historically proven or verifiable story which is passed down by tradition from earlier times and popularly accepted as historical. When you say legendary the suffix -ry (that comes from suffix -ery) means that it has the condition or role of

LEISURED: Past tense of leisure means to have a time where you do not have duties or demands for work. A time where someone can enjoy hobbies sports etc

LIGHT: To spark something with fire, to put light into something, the state of being visible exposed to view, it also means of little weight not heavy. In come of the poems it is used with one sense and in some with another

LIFE: Life is what animates, it is the spirit that gives that characteristic of existence to things.

LITERARY: Related to books and writing

MAGIC DIMENSION: A dimension is what gives the property of space to something. It can also mean an extension into something. Magic the art of producing a desired effect or result through the means that gives control and cause over the components of the natural. A magic dimension would be in that sense a space where things become unlimited and magically created no need to apply force and mechanical effort to get things done.

MAKE BELIEVE: Imaginary, pretended but in a innocent or play like pretense. A child when it plays and imagines something and assumes that role is making believe that it is that role

MANLY: It grows in strength. It is used to describe that point where the Arabic or Greek coffee is cooked and instead of boiling it grows and expands and ascends the cooker. If one will not turn off the cooker then it will spill

MARK: To give or have a distinctive trait or characteristic that gives the distinctive feature of something

MATURE: To complete in development having the characteristics of full development, something completed perfected

MASQUERADES: A false outside show a facade a pretence a disguise. It can also mean an existence under false pretenses

MAY: Expresses possibility, opportunity or permission. It can also express a wish toward something

MERRIMENT: A cheerful or joyful feeling to cause such with something

MESHED: Mesh means to connect or interlock something to combine something. In the poem it indicates and interconnection and agreement of different substances, intentions, natures. It is a game interconnecting to the way water and coffee mixes to the way the living interconnects

MUNDANE: The common ordinary, unimaginative connected to the wordly things

MYTHICAL: Without a foundation in fact, imaginary created

NOVEL: Of a new and unusual kind different from anything known or seen or experienced before.

ORIGAMI: The traditional Japanese art or technique of folding paper into a variety of decorative or represented forms as of animals or flowers

ORIGINAL: New fresh or novel, capable of or giving to thought an independent creative or individual manner

PERCEIVE: To recognize to understand to become aware of know identify by means of senses

PERUSE: To scan to read through with thoroughness or care, to examine in detail

PIECES: a separate portion or quantity of something an amount of work forming a single job

PILGRIMAGE: a long journey especially one undertaken as a quest or to pay homage to something

PLACID: pleasantly calm or peaceful tranquil

PSALM: a sacred song or hymn, a poem of a similar nature

POEM: a composition in verse like writing that express by the heightened meaning of the language or words and the rhythm express an intensively imaginative interpretation of a subject

POISES: that carries itself in that case in a particular manner

POWER: Ability to do or act ability to accomplish something a marked ability to do or act

PREVAILED: in that case exist everywhere to succeed and become dominant in something

PROVIDE: to make available, furnish to supply the means of support

PURPOSE: the reason for which something exists or is done, made, used. An aim an intention

QUIETS: make or be sound free. Free from disturbance or noise or trouble

RANSOM: the sum or price paid for deliverance from captivity or bondage

REALITY: The real things facts events one can experience in the physical world

REPEAL: to revoke or withdraw formally from something.

RESOLUTE: firmly determined set on purpose or opinion

REVOLVED: to move in a circular or curving course or orbit

RIPPLE: to form small waves in liquid or in sound waves of undulation like water moved by a breeze. When used as a verb it means to mark something as if with outgoing ripples or give a wavy form to something.

RUSTLING: to make a succession of slight soft sounds, as leaves. To cause such sounds by moving or stirring something

SCENT: a distinctive odour especially when is agreeable (like the sent of Jasmine) a perfume it also means to fill something with such odor

SCATTERING: to diffuse or deflect something sending it in many directions

SMALL BURNER: In a cooking place that works with gas a burner is that fixture that emits gas and when fired burns and cooks in that way. The small burner is the smaller of these fixtures

SAND DUST: dust means fine dry particles. Here sand dust means a speck of sand that can fly off or through like dust

SOLACE: something that gives comfort or relief something that cheers

SPARKLE: to shine be brilliant vivacious like through small gleams of light. To glitter

SPELLED: to express something correctly and clearly to explain something in an explicit way

SPIRITUALITY: the spiritual character as shown in thought etc.

SPITE: a malicious but not great desire to annoy harm frustrate or humiliate another person

STUNNING: causing astonishment in viewing something that contains a striking beauty or excellence

SUMMONED: to call for the presence of as by command, or message it also means to call into action

SUN TANNED: Tanned by the sun like the skin colour that the skin can take when exposed to the sun

SWELL: to grow in amount or force to increase in volume like the sea when it rises or a wave when it rises

TACK: a course of action or conduct especially one that is different from some other or preceding course to rurn

TEND: to move toward to lean

TENDED: past tense the action of moving toward

TEXTURE: Essence, an essential or characteristic quality

TICK: a moment or instant. Also the slight sharp recurring tick that the clock does in counting the minutes

TINKLES: to call one's attention to attract one by this sound that resembles a small bell or a keyboard instrument

TORCH: something considered like a source of illumination or guidance like a torch that illuminates through fire

TRIFLING: Light not heavy

THOUGHT: The capacity of imagining, reasoning an intention judgement or belief. The intellectual of ideas opinions

TUMBLING: to roll over, refers to big waves when they curve

TRUE: not false actual in that case

UNSCATHED: unharmed, untouched, whole

UP TO: suitable, equal to, desirable

UPSIDE: the positive side the encouraging side or result

URGE: that drive or impel that induces action

UNRULY: lawless, ungovernable

VELLUM: a texture of paper

VICIOUSNESS: cruel disposed to evil, mean

VIGOUR: effective energy or force or intensity capacity for survival, strong

VISION: sensing with the eyes, or through the mind anticipating something that will come to be

WORK: the product of one's effort

WAVELENGTH: characterized by that quality of energy that waves have. Waves can be very light or heavy

WARPED: bend or twist out of shape. In the sense used means to take them from a true or natural way or direction and bend them into the reality of the physical universe

WEAVED: to direct or move along in a winding zigzag course

WICKER: a basket made out of interweaved plant twigs

WITHIN: in or relating to the interior world in the mind in the heart

YOUTHFUL: having the appearance vigor freshness of youth

ZEPHYR: a gentle mild breeze

ZEST: hearty enjoyment, interest liveliness or energy

www.ingramcontent.com/pod-product-compliance
Lightning Source LLC
Chambersburg PA
CBHW071127130526
44590CB00056B/2890